go

Editor
DAVID E. CARTER

Book Designer
SUZANNA M.W. BROWN

The Carter Library of Design

Logos Go Digital
First published 1997 by Hearst Books International
1350 Avenue of the Americas
New York, NY 10019

ISBN: 0688-15701-7

Distributed in the U.S. and Canada by
Watson-Guptill Publications
1515 Broadway
New York, NY 10035
Tel: 800-451-1741
           908-363-4511 in NJ, AK, HI
Fax: 908-363-0338

Distributed throughout the rest of the world by
Hearst Books International
1350 Avenue of the Americas
New York, NY 10019
Fax: 212-261-6795

First published in Germany by:
NIPPAN
Nippon Shuppan Hanbai
Duetschland GmbH
Krefelder Str. 85
D-40549 Dusseldorf
Tel: (0211)5048089
Fax: (0211)5049326

ISBN: 3-931884-13-9

Copyright 1997 by Hearst Books International and David E. Carter

Printed in Hong Kong by Everbest Printing Company through
Four Colour Imports, Louisville Kentucky.

Logos
go
DIGITAL

(They don't make logos like they used to…)

No, they don't make logos like they used to. T-squares can be found in antique shops, and drawing boards make wonderful fabric cutting boards if you happen to quilt. Designers use mice (the plural of mouse) and a new era of logo design is here.

This is a very appropriate logo to open this book. Like many designs which will follow, it could not have been easily created in the PM (Pre-Macintosh) era. And, it is important that the identity is displayed here not on a page, but as a logo on a computer monitor. More and more, design decisions must consider how a logo will appear as a cyberspace image. This logo even changes color!

4

Client: BENEVIA (FORMERLY NUTRASWEET)
Designer: THE DESIGN COMPANY
            SAN FRANCISCO, CALIFORNIA

Client: PULTE HOME COPRPORATION
Designer: PARAGRAPHS DESIGN, INC.
CHICAGO, ILLINOIS

Client: JENNIFER SANDS; CRANFORD STREET
Designer: MIRES DESIGN
SAN DIEGO, CALIFORNIA

6

Client: PULTE HOME COPRPORATION
Designer: PARAGRAPHS DESIGN, INC.
CHICAGO, ILLINOIS

Client: 1996 Olympiaddy Logo
Designer: DogStar
            Birmingham, Alabama

Designer's Comments:
"Pencil sketch was scanned, converted to a computer illustration and colorized. The pencil strokes acquired a very distressed look after being converted to an illustration file. I don't think I could have achieved this effect through traditional techniques."

Client: Pulte Home Coprporation
Designer: Paragraphs Design, Inc.
            Chicago, Illinois

Client: NETLINK
Designer: ADDISON WHITNEY
CHARLOTTE, NORTH CAROLINA

Netlink

Client: NEW YORK MERCANTILE
Designer: PAGANUCCI DESIGN INC.
NEW YORK, NEW YORK

Client: DONNELLEY ENTERPRISE SOLUTIONS
Designer: MIRES DESIGN
          SAN DIEGO, CALIFORNIA

Client: CLARITY CONSULTING
Designer: DESIGN MOVES, LTD.
          WINNETKA, ILLINOIS

Client: FRESH IDEAS MAGAZINE (SECTION ICONS)
Designer: RE: SALZMAN DESIGNS
           CADYVILLE, NEW YORK

10

Client: NETSTREAM, INC.
Designer: SEMAN DESIGN
PITTSBURGH, PENNSYLVANIA

NETGAIN

Client: 1996 OLYMPIADDY LOGO
Designer: DOGSTAR
BIRMINGHAM, ALABAMA

DESIGNER'S COMMENTS:
"I probably would not have designed this logo without the aid of a computer. There would have been many, many amberlith overlays and the registration would have been almost impossible."

B R A V O • B U S

Client: RIDGE VINEYARDS
Designer: SCOTT BROWN DESIGN
            REDWOOD CITY, CALIFORNIA

Client: KIMBERLY CLARK CORPORATION
Designer: PIRMAN COMMUNICATIONS
            GREEN BAY, WISCONSIN

12

Client: FERNANDO GARCIA
Designer: HANDLER DESIGN GROUP, INC.
            WHITE PLAINS, NEW YORK

Client: CELEBRATE '98
              150TH CELEBRATION OF WOMEN'S SUFFRAGE
Designer: IN HOUSE GRAPHIC DESIGN INC.
              WATERLOO, NEW YORK

Client: CERUZZI PROPERTIES
Designer: LINCOLN DESIGN
              EUGENE, OREGON

13

Client: COMICRAFT
Designer: COMICRAFT
              SANTA MONICA, CALIFORNIA

Client: NATIONAL TOXICS CAMPAIGN
Designer: GUNNAR SWANSON DESIGN OFFICE
           DULUTH, MINNESOTA

Client: TALBOT DESIGN GROUP
Designer: TALBOT DESIGN GROUP
           WESTLAKE VILLAGE, CALIFORNIA

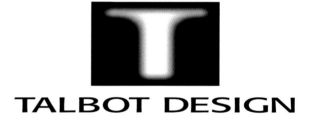

TALBOT DESIGN

Milestones

Client: MILESTONES
Designer: JULIA TAM DESIGN
           PALOS VERDES, CALIFORNIA

Client: STOLAS GROUP
Designer: SHIELDS DESIGN
           FRESNO, CALIFORNIA

Client: DATASCOPE
Designer: AERIAL
           SAN FRANCISCO, CALIFORNIA

15

Client: GST INTERNET
Designer: KEITH SASAKI
           PORTLAND, OREGON

Client: CALYPSO IMAGING
Designer: AERIAL
          SAN FRANCISCO, CALIFORNIA

Client: SPECIALTY BEERS INTERNATIONAL
16 Designer: SHIELDS DESIGN
          FRESNO, CALIFORNIA

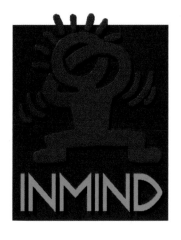

Client: INMIND
Designer: SURFPUPPY MULTIMEDIA GROUP
          TULSA, OKLAHOMA

Client: PARDNERS UNLIMITED, INC.
Designer: LOVE PACKAGING GROUP
         WICHITA, KANSAS

DESIGNER'S COMMENTS:

"We decided to do a logo that looked like a brand. The logo began with the simplest of pencil sketches. This served as reference which was not necessary to have scanned. The basic P-letterform brand was worked out in FreeHand. The paths were then exported to Illustrator and copied to the clipboard. Photoshop was opened and the paths were pasted in. They served as selections for the basic form of the P-brand. A channel was made of the brand and the Lighting Effects filter was applied using the Two O-Clock Spotlight setting with some slight adjustments. The P-brand channel was applied as the texture channel (with white as high turned OFF to achieve the deboss) before clicking OK. The P-brand channel was then used to clip out the debossed image. The image was further enhanced by layering it with a burned color layer and several layers of airbrushed smoke and shadows, which were created by carving away light gray airbrushing with layer masks. This logo was created in RGB mode and then converted to CMYK once the filtering was done. Since this logo would primarily be used in Photoshop on packaging, but also in FreeHand on the corporate ID, it was created and saved as a series of transparent layers that can be grouped in Photoshop and pulled on top of whatever background is desired. This also gave us the most versatility when it came to grayscale or color variations which could be rapidly adapted to just the right look by tweaking specific layers or only using certain ones, depending upon the application."

KENT·DELORD
HOUSE MUSEUM

Client: **KENT-DELORD HOUSE MUSEUM**
Designer: RE: SALZMAN DESIGNS
           CADYVILLE, NEW YORK

Client: **AIDS COUNCIL OF NERTHEASTERN NY**
Designer: RE: SALZMAN DESIGNS
           CADYVILLE, NEW YORK

18

AIDS COUNCIL
Northeastern New York

Client: **DENTAL GROUP OF PLATTSBURG**
Designer: RE: SALZMAN DESIGNS
           CADYVILLE, NEW YORK

Client: **EXPO**
Designer: RE: SALZMAN DESIGNS
          CADYVILLE, NEW YORK

EXPO

LAKE CHAMPLAIN
productions
INC

Client: LAKE CHAMPLAIN PRODUCTIONS
Designer: RE: SALZMAN DESIGNS
          CADYVILLE, NEW YORK

Client: NELSON PARKER (PHOTOGRAPHER)
Designer: RE: SALZMAN DESIGNS
          CADYVILLE, NEW YORK

NELS◼N
PARKER

PHO
TOG
RAP
HER

Client: Hawk's Nest Publishing
Designer: Lambert Design
           Dallas, Texas

Client: Audio Video Options
Designer: Aerial
           San Francisco, California

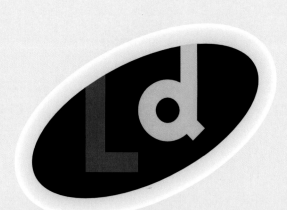

Client: Lambert Design
Designer: Lambert Design
           Dallas, Texas

Client: IDEAS + SOLUTIONS
Designer: LAMBERT DESIGN
          DALLAS, TEXAS

IDEAS AND  SOLUTIONS

TIMES
SQUARE
上海時代廣場

Client: TIMES SQUARE; SHANGHAI, CHINA
Designer: FRCH DESIGN WORLDWIDE
           CINCINNATI, OHIO

21

Client: BLAND, GARVEY, EADS, MEDLOCK + DEPPE
Designer: LAMBERT DESIGN
          DALLAS, TEXAS

Client: CORONADO CENTER
Designer: FRCH DESIGN WORLDWIDE
         CINCINNATI, OHIO

Client: BANGKOK DOME PLAZA
Designer: FRCH DESIGN WORLDWIDE
         CINCINNATI, OHIO

Client: TEMPUS ENTERTAINMENT
Designer: FRCH DESIGN WOWLDWIDE
         CINCINNATI, OHIO

Client: IMPACT UNLIMITED
Designer: AERIAL
SAN FRANCISCO, CALIFORNIA

AccuSight

Client: ACCUSIGHT
Designer: JULIA TAM DESIGN
PALOS VERDES, CALIFORNIA

23

Client: DIGITAL IMPACT
Designer: SURFPUPPY MULTIMEDIA GROUP
TULSA, OKLAHOMA

YOU DRINK. YOU DRIVE.
YOU LOSE.

Client: AUTOMOBILE CLUB OF CALIFORNIA
Designer: JULIA TAM DESIGN
          PALOS VERDES, CALIFORNIA

Client: SOUTHERN CALIFORNIA GAS CO.
Designer: JULIA TAM DESIGN
          PALOS VERDES, CALIFORNIA

24

Procurement & Logistics

Client: KMY INSTRUMENTS
Designer: JULIA TAM DESIGN
          PALOS VERDES, CALIFORNIA

Client: VOIT SPORTS
Designer: MIRES DESIGN
            SAN DIEGO, CALIFORNIA

Client: GOODS FOR GUNS
Designer: MIKE QUON DESIGN OFFICE
            NEW YORK, NEW YORK

25

Client: HELLENIC AMERICAN CRUISES
Designer: JULIA TAM DESIGN
            PALOS VERDES, CALIFORNIA

NUGGET

Client: **NUGGET**
Designer: HC DESIGN
BETHESDA, MARYLAND

Client: **CAMERAD, INC.**
Designer: SHIELDS DESIGN
FRESNO, CALIFORNIA

Client: **GLOBALGATE**
Designer: HC DESIGN
BETHESDA, MARYLAND

GLOBALGATE

Client: **NIKE; DEION SANDERS LOGO**
Designer: MIRES DESIGN
SAN DIEGO, CALIFORNIA

Client: **TOSHIBA**
Designer: MIKE QUON DESIGN OFFICE
NEW YORK, NEW YORK

27

Client: **NEXTEC**
Designer: MIRES DESIGN
SAN DIEGO, CALIFORNIA

CEBIS

CENTRAL EUROPEAN BUSINESS
INFORMATION SERVICES INC.

Client: CEBIS
Designer: HANSEN DESIGN COMPANY
            SEATTLE, WASHINGTON

Client: SONY
Designer: MIKE QUON DESIGN OFFICE
            NEW YORK, NEW YORK

Client: DIGITAL IMAGING
Designer: HANSEN DESIGN COMPANY
            SEATTLE, WASHINGTON

Client: THE LOOP CORPORATION
Designer: HANSEN DESIGN COMPANY
           SEATTLE, WASHSINGTON

Client: UNISTAR
Designer: MIKE QUON DESIGN OFFICE
           NEW YORK, NEW YORK

29

Client: eMEDIA ENTERTAINMENT COMPANY
Designer: HANSEN DESIGN COMPANY
           SEATTLE, WASHINGTON

Client: **NIKE; CROSS TRAINING**
Designer: MIRES DESIGN
SAN DIEGO, CALIFORNIA

Client: **MATT RHODE, PIANIST**
Designer: KEILER DESIGN GROUP
FARMINGTON, CONNECTICUT

30

Client: **NIKE; MICHAEL JORDAN**
Designer: MIRES DESIGN
SAN DIEGO, CALIFORNIA

Client: TSUNAMI DIVE GEAR
Designer: MIRES DESIGN
          SAN DIEGO, CALIFORNIA

Client: CALIFORNIA CENTER FOR THE ARTS
Designer: MIRES DESIGN
          SAN DIEGO, CALIFORNIA

Client: ITALIAN HOTEL RESERVATION CENTER
Designer: JULIA TAM DESIGN
          PALOS VERDES, CALIFORNIA

Client: **KEILER ONLINE; KEILER & COMPANY**
Designer: **KEILER NEW MEDIA**
FARMINGTON, CONNECTICUT

DESIGNER'S COMMENTS:
"We needed an identity for our New Media work and started with our current logo, a 2-D 'K'. Next, we extruded 2-D illustrator eps artwork in Strate Studio Pro. We then rasterized the 'online' type in Photoshop and used it as a transparency mask on a rotating cylinder. After creating this 3-D logo, we wanted to take it to the next level—animating it and using it on our website. First we exported PICS animation into Macromedia Director for conversion to Shockwave document. Next, we embedded the dcr file into an HTML web page."

32

Client: **ORTHODONTIC ASSOCIATES**
Designer: **SUSAN NORTHROP DESIGN**
PROVIDENCE, RHODE ISLAND

Client: FOUND STUFF
Designer: MIRES DESIGN
           SAN DIEGO, CALIFORNIA

Client: BREW HAHA; THE FOOD GROUP
Designer: MIRES DESIGN
           SAN DIEGO, CALIFORNIA

33

Client: THE CAPE; MTM ENTERTAINMENT
Designer: MIKE SALISBURY COMMUNICATIONS, INC.
           TORRANCE, CALIFORNIA

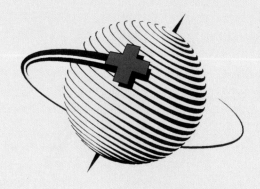

Client: NATIONAL PHYSICIANS NETWORK
Designer: WHITE DESIGN
           LONG BEACH, CALIFORNIA

Client: PLANET 1
Designer: HC DESIGN
           BETHESDA, MARYLAND

Client: BARRINGTON CONSULTING GROUP
Designer: WHITE DESIGN
           LONG BEACH, CALIFORNIA

Client: THE SURFARIS
Designer: GENE BERRYHILL PRODUCTIONS
           LAGUNA BEACH, CALIFORNIA

DESIGNER'S COMMENTS:
"Step by step design process:
1. In Photoshop I made a solid color background.
2. Noise was added from the filter menu and then gaussian was selected.
3. From Illustrator, a black and white version of the logo was imported (hand drawing of the logo was scanned, outlined and filled).
4. The floating selection (logo) was dragged into the new layer icon and preserve transparency was chosen.
5. Next, the move tool was used to nudge the top logo layer slightly to create a shadow.
6. Emboss was applied from the filter menu and overlay was selected from the layers palette to display the background color and texture of the logo.
7. The edges were blurred by first selecting the preserve transparency box, then gaussian blur was added through filters, blur. Radius: 2.
8. The background layer was selected, then the noise filter, adding noise. Other options: 20, gaussian, monochromatic.
9. The last step was applied with the airbrush tool adding highlights and shading."

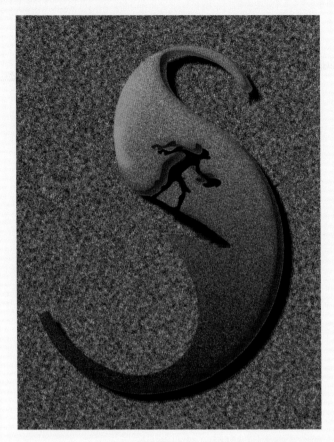

Client: UUCOM, INC.
Designer: THE INVISIONS GROUP LTD.
           BETHESDA, MARYLAND

Client: 103.7—THE PLANET RADIO STATION
Designer: CAPENER, MATTHEWS & WALCHER
                   SAN DIEGO, CALIFORNIA
Illustrator: TRACY SABIN

Client: STUFF-IT
Designer: MIKE SALISBURY COMMUNICATIONS, INC.
                   TORRANCE, CALIFORNIA

36

Client: THE PHANTOM; PARAMOUNT PICTURES
Designer: MIKE SALISBURY COMMUNICATIONS, INC.
                   TORRANCE, CALIFORNIA

Client: ANGELS LOGO; THE WALT DIENEY CO.
Designer: MIKE SALISBURY COMMUNICATIONS, INC.
            TORRANCE, CALIFONIA

Client: POWER HOUSE LOGO; STAT HOUSE
Designer: MIKE SALISBURY COMMUNICATIONS, INC.
            TORRANCE, CALIFORNIA

Client: RAGE MAGAZINE
Designer: MIKE SALISBURY COMMUNICATIONS, INC.
            TORRANCE, CALIFONIA

STOTT
& ASSOCIATES

Client: STOTT & ASSOCIATES
Designer: MICKELSON DESIGN
            AMES, IOWA

Client: DIGITAL DOMAIN
Designer: MIKE SALISBURY COMMUNICAITONS, INC.
            TORRANCE CA

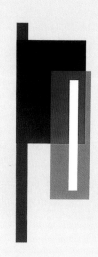

Web
Elite

Client: WEB ELITE
Designer: THE COMARK GROUP
            DETROIT, MICHIGAN

Client: AMERICAN SOCIETY OF FURNITURE DESIGNERS
Designer: MICEKLSON, DESIGN
AMES, IOWA

Client: WESTERN WATER INTERNATIONAL
FRIGIPURE
Designer: STEVE TRAPERO DESIGN
SILVER SPRING, MARYLAND

39

Client: ACCURATE AUTOMOTIVE INTERIORS
Designer: MICKELSON DESIGN
AMES, IOWA

Client: **RAGE MAGAZINE**
Designer: **MIKE SALISBURY COMMUNICATIONS, INC.**
TORRANCE, CALIFORNIA

Client: **HARMONY BUSINESS MACHINES**
40   Designer: MICKELSON DESIGN
AMES, IOWA

Client: **BOY SCOUTS OF AMERICA;**
BROKEN ARROW DISTRICT
Designer: MICKELSON DESIGN
AMES, IOWA

Client: CHAOS LURES
Designer: MIRES DESIGN
            SAN DIEGO, CALIFORNIA
Illustrator: TRACY SABIN

41

Client: SEAU'S—THE RESTAURANT
Designer: TRACY SABIN GRAPHIC DESIGN
           SAN DIEGO, CALIFORNIA

Client: CATNIP GARDEN
Designer: LOVE PACKAGING GROUP
           WICHITA, KANSAS

Client: AMERICAN GARDEN COLLECTION
Designer: LOVE PACKAGING GROUP
            WICHITA, KANSAS

DESIGNER'S COMMENTS:
"The American Garden Collection product trademark was
created for the Hayes Co., which manufactures all types of
lawn and garden products.

"This was first illustrated with marker on tracing paper; the
black & white image was scanned and manipulated in
Photoshop 3.0.5. The B&W art was airbrushed to develop
the basic color you see in the finished logo. To give the logo a
warm, weathered look, a piece of plywood was scanned as
grayscale. The wood scan was adjusted with levels to create a
high contrast image on the woodgrain. A selection of the
woodgrain was copied onto a new layer above the colored logo.
The selection was filled with white and opacity set to 125%,
making a very subtle, light woodgrain effect in the dark
areas. Then, that layer was duplicated and filled with a
dark brown with opacity at 20%, and layer function on
multiply, making a subtle, dark grain in the light areas."

43

Client: WILDLIFE FOUNDATION OF FLORIDA
Designer: SYNERGY DESIGN GROUP
            TALLAHASSEE, FLORIDA

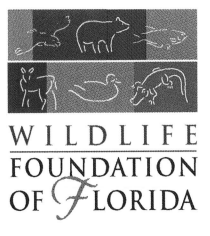

Client: HOLDEMAN'S TOTAL LAWN CARE SERVICE
Designer: INSIGHT DESIGN COMMUNICATIONS
WICHITA, KANSAS

DESIGNER'S COMMENTS:
"This logo began as a rough sketch that was scanned and placed onto a background layer in Freehand. Then with the pin tool, the logo was drawn in a foreground layer like cutting amberlith over a pencil sketch for a guide. Working in the computer made it easy to keep consistent spacing in lines and shapes. Furthermore, the 'H' was extended and made rough with the Freehand tweak function."

44

Client: MAULDIN AUTOMOTIVE REPAIR
Designer: MICKELSON DESIGN
AMES, IOWA

Client: PRO PAC
Designer: INSIGHT DESIGN COMMUNICATIONS
WICHITA, KANSAS

DESIGNER'S COMMENTS:
"This logo took about 15 minutes to produce once the idea was conceived. The logo consisted of a simple circle and lines for the 'P's/package."

Client: COLLEGIATE SCHOOL;
           30TH HOMECOMING CELEBRATION
Designer: LOVE PACKAGING GROUP
           WICHITA, KANSAS

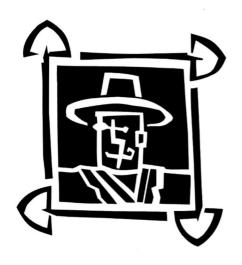

Client: COLLEGIATE SCHOOL;
           FOUNDERS DAY CELEBRATION
Designer: LOVE PACKAGING GROUP
           WICHITA, KANSAS

Client: LOVE BOX CO. GRAPHICS DEPT.
Designer: LOVE PACKAGING GROUP
          WICHITA, KANSAS

Client: LOVE BOX CO. SALES SERVICE
Designer: LOVE PACKAGING GROUP
          WICHITA, KANSAS

Client: HARCOURT BRACE & CO.
Designer: MIRES DESIGN
            SAN DIEGO, CALIFORNIA
Illustrator: TRACY SABIN

47

Client: CITY OF CEDAR RAPIDS
Designer: MICKELSON DESIGN
           AMES, IOWA

Client: MIRES DESIGN
Designer: MIRES DESIGN
           SAN DIEGO, CALIFORNIA
Illustrator: TRACY SABIN

Client: NIKE; DEION SANDERS LOGO
Designer: MIRES DESIGN
          SAN DIEGO, CALIFORNIA
Illustrator:TRACY SABIN

49

Client: BRAINSTORM
Designer: ATELIER
          PALO ALTO, CALIFORNIA

Client: FOUND STUFF PAPERWORKS
Designer: MIRES DESIGN
                 SAN DIEGO, CALIFORNIA
Illustrator: TRACY SABIN

50

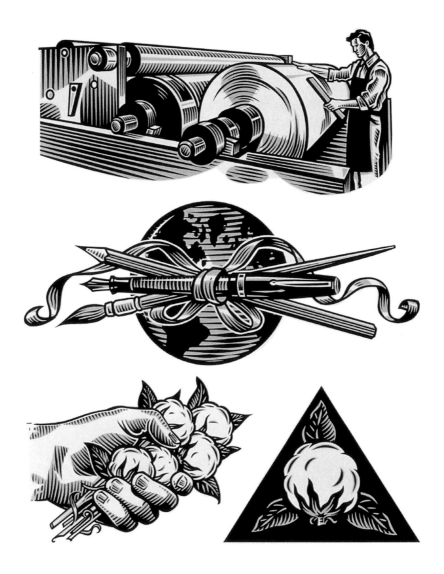

Client: CITY OF CEDAR RAPIDS
Designer: MICKELSON DESIGN
        AMES, IOWA

Client: MONT & RUTH 50TH ANNIVERSARY
Designer: MICKELSON DESIGN
        AMES, IOWA

51

Client: CITY OF CEDAR RAPIDS
Designer: MICKELSON DESIGN
        AMES, IOWA

Client: UNIVERSITY TOWNE CENTER
Designer: TRACY SABIN GRAPHIC DESIGN
          SAN DIEGO, CALIFORNIA

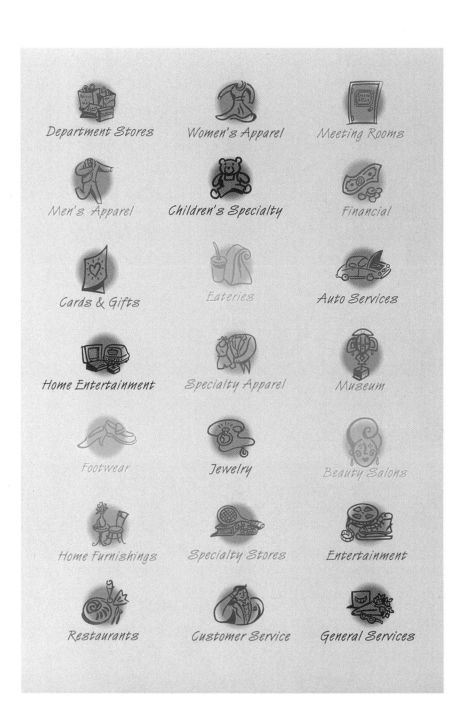

Client: **FREELANCE PRODUCTIONS**
Designer: TRACY SABIN GRAPHIC DESIGN
SAN DIEGO, CALIFORNIA

Client: **MCMILLIN COMMUNITIES**
Designer: MIRES DESIGN
SAN DIEGO, CALIFORNIA
Illustrator: TRACY SABIN

Client: **HASTINGS FILTERS INC.**
Designer: LOVE PACKAGING GROUP
WICHITA, KANSAS

DESIGNER'S COMMENTS:
"The logo proposed for Hastings Filters Inc. began in FreeHand where the scalloped edge was created by using the polygon tool, and then selecting all points on the shape and choosing curve as the point type, and automatic for the bezier handles—instant scallops. Next, all paths were exported to Illustrator and copied to the clipboard. Photoshop was opened and the paths were pasted in along with the pixels. The first layer was duplicated and the GE chrome filter was applied. This layers mode was set at soft light. This duplication chromes (and one layer with GE plaster) layer mode setting process was repeated until the right look was achieved. The final step was to go to selective color and bring back some of the color in the bottom layer that at this point was appearing knocked back by the multilayer compositing. The contrast was increased in layers and a flattened version of the logo was saved in addition to the layered one."

54

Client: **AGASSI ENTERPRISES**
Designer: MIRES DESIGN
SAN DIEGO, CALIFORNIA

Client: SAN DIEGO GAS & ELECTRIC
             (COYOTE DIVISION)
Designer: FRANKLIN-STOORZA
             SAN DIEGO, CALIFORNIA
Illustrator: TRACY SABIN

Client: HARCOURT BRACE & CO.
Designer: MIRES DESIGN
             SAN DIEGO, CALIFORNIA
Illustrator: TRACY SABIN

Client: SAN DIEGO OPERA
Designer: TRACY SABIN GRAPHIC DESIGN
SAN DIEGO, CALIFORNIA

Client: TURNER ENTERTAINMENT CO.
Designer: TRACY SABIN GRAPHIC DESIGN
SAN DIEGO, CALIFORNIA

Client: **TURNER ENTERTAINMENT CO.**
Designer: **TRACY SABIN GRAPHIC DESIGN**
          SAN DIEGO, CALIFORNIA

Client: **THE FRANKLIN MINT**
Designer: **SARGENT & BERMAN**
          SANTA MONICA, CALIFORNIA

Client: LINCOLN PARK ZOO
Designer: TRACY SABIN GRAPHIC DESIGN
SAN DIEGO, CALIFORNIA

58

Client: GOLDLINE
Designer: MIRES DESIGN
SAN DIEGO, CALFORNIA
Illustrator: TRACY SABIN

Client: LINCOLN PARK ZOO
Designer: TRACY SABIN GRAPHIC DESIGN
SAN DIEGO, CALIFORNIA

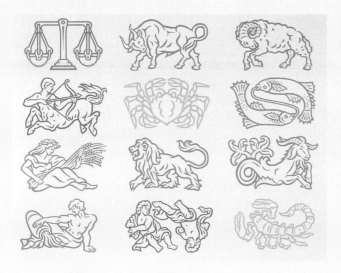

Client: CRANFORD STREET
Designer: MIRES DESIGN
             SAN DIEGO, CALIFORNIA
Illustrator: TRACY SABIN

Client: McMILLIN COMMUNITIES
Designer: MIRES DESIGN
             SAN DIEGO, CALIFORNIA
Illustrator: TRACY SABIN

Client: **BIG WEENIE RECORDS**
Designer: TRACY SABIN GRAPHIC DESIGN
SAN DIEGO, CALIFORNIA

Client: **ALMOND BOARD OF CALIFORNIA**
Designer: FOOTE, CONE & BELDING
SAN FRANCISCO, CALIFORNIA
Illustrator: **TRACY SABIN**

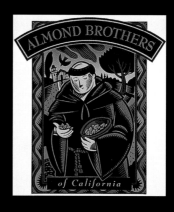

Client: **THE GRIPPER**
Designer: MIRES DESIGN
SAN DIEGO, CALIFORNIA
Illustrator: **TRACY SABIN**

Client: CRANFORD DESIGN
Designer: MIRES DESIGN
          SAN DIEGO, CALIFORNIA
Illustrator: TRACY SABIN

Client: ADVANCED CARDIOVASCULAR SYSTEMS
Designer: MIRES DESIGN
          SAN DIEGO, CALIFORNIA
Illustrator: TRACY SABIN

Client: ADVANCED CARDIOVASCULAR SYSTEMS
Designer: MIRES DESIGN
           SAN DIEGO, CALIFORNIA
Illustrator: TRACY SABIN

Client: SERVUS HOTEL GROUP
Designer: IN HOUSE GRAPHIC DESIGN, INC.
           WATERLOO, NEW YORK

Client: Calypso Software Systems
Designer: Tracy Sabin Graphic Design
           San Diego, California

Client: Harcourt Brace & Co.
Designer: Mires Design
            San Diego, California
Illustrator: Tracy Sabin

63

Client: Pompano Square
Designer: Tracy Sabin Graphic Design
           San Diego, California

ASCENT

Client: **ASCENT ENTERTAINMENT GROUP**
Designer: **THE GRAPHIC EXPRESSION, INC.**
            NEW YORK, NEW YORK

64

Client: **YOUNG AT ART**
Designer: **THE GRAPHIC EXPRESSION, INC.**
            NEW YORK, NEW YORK

GATEWAY

Client: GATEWAY INSURANCE COMPANY
Designer: THE GRAPHIC EXPRESSION, INC.
          NEW YORK, NEW YORK

Conti*Financial*

Client: CONTI FINANCIAL SERVICES
Designer: THE GRAPHIC EXPRESSION, INC.
          NEW YORK, NEW YORK

Client: CARDIO THORACIC SYSTEMS
Designer: THE GRAPHIC EXPRESSION
          NEW YORK, NEW YORK

Client: HOT ROD HELL
Designer: MIRES DESIGN
            SAN DIEGO, CALIFORNIA
Illustrator: TRACY SABIN

66

Client: CRAMER CALLIGRAPHY
Designer: LOVE PACKAGING GROUP
          WICHITA, KANSAS

DESIGNER'S COMMENTS:

"This is a logo that could have been tough, but was made very easy thanks to the spiral X-tra tool in FreeHand. After initial sketches gave me the look I was aiming for, I had to find a way to achieve a smooth spiraling C letter form. The FreeHand spiral X-tra tool was a wonderfully easy way to get my initial spiral line, which is simply cloned and rotated to achieve the thicks and thins of the C. I created the C in a top half and a bottom half, since I wanted them to not be symmetrical, and joined them when I had their thicknesses adjusted. The rest of the elements that make up this logo were clicked out with the Freehand pen tool in a matter of minutes."

Client: HOC INDUSTRIES
Designer: LOVE PACKAGING GROUP
          WICHITA, KANSAS

DESIGNER'S COMMENTS:

"After pencil sketches resolved the basics of the three logos, the sketches were scanned and put on their own layers in FreeHand to serve as reference. The line art was traced and fine-tuned and then exported to Illustrator where it was copied to the clipboard and then pasted into Photoshop as paths. Since a cubist-type look was desired, Photoshop's layers were a dream to work with. Each airbrushed section got its own layer and the paths were turned to selections and offset to serve as airbrushing friskets. When the logos were completed, they were flattened and saved as grayscale Tiff files and imported into FreeHand as needed."

The logo image (circular seal) reads:

N·O·R·T·H·F·I·E·L·D
S·C·H·O·O·L
with outer ring text: MUSIC · ARITHMETIC · LOGIC · RHETORIC · ASTRONOMY · GEOMETRY · POETICS

Client: NORTHFIELD SCHOOL
Designer: LOVE PACKAGING GROUP
               WICHITA, KANSAS

DESIGNER'S COMMENTS:

"After a pencil sketch resolved the basics of the logo, the sketch was scanned and put on its own layer in FreeHand to serve as reference. The line art was traced, fine-tuned, and then exported to Illustrator where it was copied to the clipboard and subsequently pasted into Photoshop as paths and as pixels. I had reillustrated the sun/clouds image, based on a vintage old advertising cut from a copyright-free book, and scanned it into Photoshop to place in the Freehand file that had been converted to a Photoshop file. The illustration remained on its own transparent layer while color was airbrushed in on lower layers. The exterior ring was done with KPT 3.0 gradient designer (gradient on paths), as this was a very fast way to achieve a rounded ring effect, rather than have a plain flat line. The variations function was utilized to begin adjusting the color on specific layers. Then a merged copy on layer of its own was created to experiment with the color fine-tuning in levels. A black background was added (to match the logo's edge) and a clipping path was created from the original pasted-in paths, so that the logo would trim out neatly for use in page layout applications. The whole advantage of doing this logo on the computer was the unlimited amount of experimenting and fine-tuning that was possible."

68

Client: WORLD WRAPPS
Designer: DESIGN ONE
           SAN FRANCISCO, CALIFORNIA

Client: ELOGEN, INC.
Designer: LOVE PACKAGING GROUP
          WICHITA, KANSAS

DESIGNER'S COMMENTS:
"This logo originated as a pencil sketch to refine the concept and see if it would work. The product is a skin care line developed by a cellular biologist who was engineering the ingredients of this product on a molecular level. This is his unique niche, so the molecular concept was solidified into a visual by taking the ingredients of the product and mapping them onto two molecules linked by the initial of the name (Elogen). The first step was to set the type for the ingredients in FreeHand, then convert to outlines and export to Illustrator. From Illustrator, the outline type was copied and pasted into a Photoshop RGB file as paths which were activated as a selection and filled with black. A circular selection was made over the ingredient list and the process was repeated over a different segment of the ingredient list to produce the other sphere/molecule. After the molecules were complete, a path for the E letterform was pasted into the file by the same method as the ingredient list. With the E on its own layer, the spheres/molecules were positioned. The final step was to colorize the logo. This was done by going into variations in Photoshop and getting in the ballpark of the target color. Finally the color was fine-tuned in levels. To achieve the different colors for different uses of the logo, the info palette in Photoshop was closely observed to insure that although the colors are different, their values are the same to make them still look like part of the same family. Any inconsistencies in value were corrected in levels."

Client: WICHITA PUBLIC SCHOOLS/
           WICHITA AREA TECHNICAL COLLEGE
Designer: LOVE PACKAGING GROUP
           WICHITA, KANSAS

70

Client: THE COFFEE MILLERS
Designer: LOVE PACKAGING GROUP
           WICHITA, KANSAS

DESIGNER'S COMMENTS:

"The Coffee Millers logo was created by scanning a pretty well-refined sketch and importing it into FreeHand. It was placed on its own layer beneath the foreground layer, so that tracing over it would go faster than if it was sent to the background. The line work was refined until the logo looked finished, but I knew it could have more impact in one color if I added some interesting screening. To do this, I exported the paths from FreeHand to Illustrator, copied them to the clipboard and pasted them into Photoshop. Once in Photoshop, the paths served as selections which I used like friskets to airbrush with. The grayscale airbrushing was converted to bitmap via a very low line screen using a huge round dot, to achieve a Ben Day-type dot screen. This screen file was then saved as a Tiff and imported back into Freehand where it was turned transparent and given a tint value of the ONE color that the logo was printed in. I could have composited the whole image in Photoshop, but by having the screen file separate, I have more options should the need arise."

Client: LOVE BOX CO. MANUFACTURING
Designer: LOVE PACKAGING GROUP
WICHITA, KANSAS

NEW MEDIA TEAMS AND TALENT

Client: MONTAGE
Designer: TEAMDESIGN, INC.
SEATTLE, WASHINGTON

Client: WEDESIGN
Designer: WHITNEY•EDWARDS GRAPHIC DESIGN
EASTON, MARYLAND

A Geographic Technologies Company

COMMUNITY
THRIFT STORE

Client: COMMUNITY THRIFT STORE
Designer: THE DESIGN FOUNDRY
          MADISON, WISCONSIN

Client: SOUTH PACIFIC ORCHID GARDENS
72 Designer: TALBOT DESIGN GROUP
          WESTLAKE VILLAGE, CALIFORNIA

Client: SPIRITUS
Designer: THE DESIGN FOUNDRY
          MADISON, WISCONSIN

Client: **LEE KUAN YEW EXCHANGE FELLOWSHIP**
Designer: **DESIGN OBJECTIVES PTE LTD.**
          SINGAPORE

LEE KUAN YEW
EXCHANGE
FELLOWSHIP

Client: **FAR EAST ORGANIZATION**
Designer: KINGGRAPHIC
          HONG KONG

73

Client: JITTERS ALL NIGHT COFFEE SHOP
Designer: INSIGHT DESIGN COMMUNICATIONS
                 WICHITA, KANSAS

DESIGNER'S COMMENTS:
"This logo was first a semi-rough sketch on tracing paper. The image was scanned and converted to paths in Streamline, then placed into FreeHand. In FreeHand the tweak function was used to create a chunky hand-done look."

74

Client: GRENE VISION GROUP
           EYE CARE ON CALL
Designer: INSIGHT DESIGN COMMUNICATIONS
                 WICHITA, KANSAS

DESIGNER'S COMMENTS:
"A semi-rough sketch on tracing paper, the image was scanned and placed into a background layer and redrawn in a foreground layer of Freehand. In Freehand, curves and circles were dissected and rearranged to develop the exact shapes and curves desired. Parts of one shape were duplicated and rotated to create other shapes. For example, both arms and legs are all modifications of the first one drawn."

Client: OFFICE AUTOMATION
Designer: INSIGHT DESIGN COMMUNICATIONS
          WICHITA, KANSAS

DESIGNER'S COMMENTS:
"This symbol was drawn in FreeHand as black-and-white vector art, exported to Illustrator and opened in Photoshop. In Photoshop, multiple layers and filters were used to create a stone-and-chrome effect. The stone effect around the type was done by applying the clouds filter, then the GE emboss filter. The chrome effect was done by applying the GE chrome filter on one layer and the plaster filter on another layer. Each layer was adjusted with opacity to allow all layers to show through at different intensities. Finally the logo was converted into a duotone."

75

Client: HOST MARRIOTT CORPORATION
Designer: THE INVISIONS GROUP LTD.
          BETHESDA, MARYLAND

HOST MARRIOTT
CORPORATION

76

Client: RAYTHEON
Designer: INSIGHT DESIGN COMMUNICATIONS
              WICHITA, KANSAS

DESIGNER'S COMMENTS:
"This is Raytheon's logo identity system encompassing infrastructure, government, power, pharmaceuticals, metals, transportation, fabrication, nuclear, polymers, and chemicals.

"This identity began as rough sketches that were scanned and placed onto a background layer in FreeHand. Then with the pen tool, the logos were drawn in a foreground layer like cutting amberlith over a pencil sketch for a guide. Working in the computer made it easy to keep consistent spacing of lines and shapes. Furthermore, variations and modifications were quickly accessible and were invaluable in achieving the final product."

Client: HOC INDUSTRIES
Designer: LOVE PACKAGING GROUP
             WICHITA, KANSAS

DESIGNER'S COMMENTS:
"The two Ultimate Protection logos were created in a very similar fashion. The Ultimate Seal (circular) logo took a little more airbrushing and masking inside of Photoshop. Both logos started as loose pencil sketches which were taped to the monitor to serve as reference as they were fleshed out in FreeHand. The banners were rendered in Dimensions and composited in FreeHand with the type and shape paths. Next, all the paths for these logos were exported to Illustrator where they were copied to the clipboard and pasted into Photoshop as pixels, then as paths. (The paths would later serve as headstarts for isolating certain areas with selections during filtering or airbrushing.) The images were color-enhanced in levels, then duplicated to another layer. This new layer was filtered with GE chrome and blended down on top of the bottom color layer using the soft light layer mode. More duplicates of the chrome layer were added and different layer modes were experimented with to enhance the sheen. The find edges filter was then applied to one of the chrome layers to really put a shine on it. At this point, any elements that needed extra enhancing were selected with the magic wand and airbrushed or given extra filtering and color enhancing. Both files contained multiple layers, so layered versions were saved in case of revisions along with flattened versions with clipping paths for placing in layout programs."

Client: PHOTO GRAPHIX
Designer: OUT OF MY MIND, VISUAL COMMUNICATIONS
               FLOSSMOOR, ILLINOIS

DESIGNER'S COMMENTS:

"Step one was to create a circle shape in Photoshop and by using the blur filters, define a gaussian blur that was a suitable vignette. I used the printer options setup menus in Photoshop to customize a very coarse line screen for printing on a 600 x 600 dpi black-and-white printer. Then printed the image as large as possible on a 8-1/2" x 11", high quality piece of paper. This involved a good deal of fine tuning (about 30 sheets) to get the dots to be geometrically uniform, and as minimal in number as possible to offer the mark an air of simplicity.

"I took the printout and scanned it into Photoshop as a 1200 dpi line scan. Despite the fact that I performed a line-art scan, the image is still defined as a rasterized image. Rasterized images work great for photographic images, but do not provide the clean crisp edge that a linear file offers.

PHOTOGRAPHIX

"After saving the Photoshop file as a tiff, I opened the file in Streamline. The auto trace function produced decent results, but there would have to be some additional fine tuning done in Illustrator to make the graphic image perfect.

78 *"Now that the image was defined as a linear file, next came the painstaking process of cleaning up the individual dot shapes that created the halftoned appearance, one by one. By adjusting the nodes and handles provided as a function of the program, deleting and sometimes adding nodes, I was able to fine tune each shape to match the appearance of the original laser. Since digital photography works as an RGB process, it seemed only natural to create a radial vignette using the colors red, green, and blue. After choosing a suitable red, green, and blue, it was a simple matter of playing around with the gradient tool in Illustrator and adjusting the balance of the color blends to my liking.*

"The graphic image of the aperture was a bit easier to execute being that it was made of entirely straight lines and I could finish it entirely in Illustrator. Since the final shape comprised a circle, and nine 'aperture blades' seemed to look best for graphic appeal, I determined the exact angle of one of the sections by dividing into 360°. Next I created one master construction shape, basically a long, thin rectangle, that had a pivot point defined by a node, about halfway down its length. Then using the angular degree determined earlier, I simply copied the element, rotated the copy using this angle, aligning the center end of the copied rectangle directly over the pivot node of the former rectangle. After copying and rotating eight more times, my aperture shape was constructed, but not yet complete. In order for it to work in the mark, it had to be one linear shape, not nine independent rectangles. I selected the entire group of rectangles and turned them into guides. I now had a perfectly defined template that I could simply trace using the ruling pen tool. Once traced, the original nine rectangular guides were deleted, leaving me with the aperture shape as a linear object that I could place over the other graphic image and fill as I pleased.

"The completion of the mark was a matter of defining a similar version of the gradient vignettes of red, green, and blue used earlier, but using white in the center to make the aperture appear open somewhat. By playing with the settings in the gradient setup, it wasn't long before I was able to align the radial blends between images to create the illusion that the blades of the aperture faded away as they moved away from center.

"I could now easily create a black-and-white version of the logo, as well as provide my client with a fairly complex image, completely in a linear format. This would insure that its quality would remain constant whether he chose to reproduce it at one inch in diameter or three feet."

Client: CROSSROADS RECORDS, INC.
Designer: DEVER DESIGNS
LAUREL, MARYLAND

Client: DIRT
Designer: JOHN VANCE
ARLINGTON, VIRGINIA

DESIGNER'S COMMENTS:
"The mark was created in Adobe Illustrator 5.0, using precise linework on a tight grid. One spike was rendered, then moved and repeated. The composition was then duplicated and flipped. Finally, the result was horizontally scaled out, and the type was added."

Client: ROCK ISLAND STUDIOS VIDEO PRODUCTION
Designer: INSIGHT DESIGN COMMUNICATIONS
WICHITA, KANSAS

80

Client: VICTORY IN THE VALLEY
CANCER PATIENT CARE
Designer: INSIGHT DESIGN COMMUNICATIONS
WICHITA, KANSAS

DESIGNER'S COMMENTS:
"This logo was drawn in Freehand and exported to Illustrator and opened in Photoshop where it was airbrushed to create the 3-D effect of the ribbon."

Client:　　HASTINGS FILTERS
Designer:　LOVE PACKAGING GROUP
　　　　　　WICHITA, KANSAS

DESIGNER'S COMMENTS:
"Hastings Filters manufactures filters for all types of vehicles.

"Hastings Quality Symbol is very simple, but would have been very difficult to produce without the use of computers. The wave circle might have taken four hours, the curved type another hour and forget about the chrome effect. The chrome effect was achieved in Photoshop using GE chrome and plaster filters on different layers and different opacities. In total the logo was created in about two hours."

Client:　　SWAN BROTHERS DAIRY
Designer:　LOVE PACKAGING GROUP
　　　　　　WICHITA, KANSAS

DESIGNER'S COMMENTS:
"This logo was first a semi-rough sketch on tracing paper. The image was scanned and converted to paths; then placed into FreeHand. In FreeHand, the type was added and converted to paths. Using the tweak function, the paths were adjusted to create a chunky hand-done look."

Client: **MENTAL HEALTH ASSOCIATION**
Designer: LOVE PACKAGING GROUP
WICHITA, KANSAS

DESIGNER'S COMMENTS:
"This logo was created using traditional amberlith, scanned, and placed into Freehand where the tiff was instantly made to thrust forward."

82

Client: **MIXOLOGY**
Designer: INSIGHT DESIGN COMMUNICATIONS
WICHITA, KANSAS

DESIGNER'S COMMENTS:
"This logo started as a chunky woodcut illustration which was scanned and placed in Freehand. The type was added and the black-and-white image was converted to paths before being exported to Illustrator. The image was then opened in Photoshop where the white areas were illustrated in color with the airbrush tool. The black woodcut line work and type were duplicated on another layer and offset slightly. Then various shades of gold were airbrushed over the black."

Client: PRAIRIE PRINT
Designer: INSIGHT DESIGN COMMUNICATIONS
              WICHITA, KANSAS

DESIGNER'S COMMENTS:
"The Prairie Print logo began as a rough black-and-white sketch which was scanned and placed into Freehand in the background layer. The wheat was drawn in pieces of lines. The lines were duplicated and then joined so the curves all related to one another."

Client: BIG DOG CUSTOM MOTORCYCLES INC.
Designer: INSIGHT DESIGN COMMUNICATIONS
              WICHITA, KANSAS

DESIGNER'S COMMENTS:
"A rough sketch of the logo was scanned and placed onto a background layer in Freehand. With the pen tool in Freehand, I drew half the logo (except the dog and type) duplicated it, mirrored it and joined the lines into exactly symmetrical shapes."

Client: RUBIOS
Designer: MIRES DESIGN
            SAN DIEGO, CALIFORNIA

Client: DARK HORSE CLOTHING CO.
Designer: DAVID LEMLEY DESIGN
            SEATTLE, WASHINGTON

DESIGNER'S COMMENTS:

84   *"As a classically trained logo artist/designer (who owns boxes of French curves, rapidiographs, triangles, and crates full of Strathmore 2-ply, 100% Rag Bristol Vellum on which to create and perfect my designs) having embraced the computer with an open heart and much enthusiasm for future technology, I felt it my duty to include the following editorial along with my entries.*

Client: TECHNOIDS
Designer: KIMURA DESIGN
            ANCHORAGE, ALASKA

Client: ROYAL CARIBBEAN
Designer: DAVID LEMLEY DESIGN
          SEATTLE, WASHINGTON

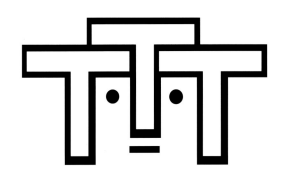

Client: DIRK MYNATT
Designer: DAVID LEMLEY DESIGN
          SEATTLE, WASHINGTON

85

Client: SEATTLE ORGANIZING COMMITTEE OF
           NCAA FINAL FOUR 1995
Designer: DAVID LEMLEY DESIGN
          SEATTLE, WASHINGTON

Client: MUZAK
Designer: DAVID LEMLEY DESIGN
           SEATTLE, WASHINGTON

Client: ACTIVE VOICE

Designer: DAVID LEMLEY DESIGN
           SEATTLE, WASHINGTON

Client: INTEL
           OGILVY MATHER
Designer: DAVID LEMLEY DESIGN
           SEATTLE, WASHINGTON

Client: MICROSOFT
Designer: DAVID LEMLEY DESIGN
              SEATTLE, WASHINGTON

Client: ALDUS CORPORATION
Designer: DAVID LEMLEY DESIGN
              SEATTLE, WASHINGTON

87

Client: MICROSOFT
Designer: DAVID LEMLEY DESIGN
              SEATTLE, WASHINGTON

Client: **B-WILD**
Designer: **DAVID LEMLEY DESIGN**
           SEATTLE, WASHINGTON

Client: **NINTENDO**
           LEIMER/CROSS

88 Designer: **DAVID LEMLEY DESIGN**
           SEATTLE, WASHINGTON

Client: **O'BRIEN INTERNATIONAL**
Designer: **DAVID LEMLEY DESIGN**
           SEATTLE, WASHINGTON

DESIGNER'S COMMENTS:
"Logo was created in Illustrator, exported into Photoshop and blurred using motion blur. Then it was imported into FreeHand where the final touches were created."

Client: ACTIVE VOICE
Designer: DAVID LEMLEY DESIGN
            SEATTLE, WASHINGTON

GEEKBŌY

Client: DAVID LEMLEY DESIGN
Designer: DAVID LEMLEY DESIGN
            SEATTLE, WASHINGTON

89

Client: DAVID LEMLEY DESIGN
Designer: DAVID LEMLEY DESIGN
            SEATTLE, WASHINGTON

Client: **DAVID LEMLEY DESIGN**
Designer: **DAVID LEMLEY DESIGN**
            SEATTLE, WASHINGTON

DESIGNER'S COMMENTS:
"Logo was created in FreeHand by rendering calligraphic letterforms with the pressure sensitive tool, controlling it with the arrow keys (as opposed to a wacom tablet) in order to achieve a deconstructionist feeling."

Client: **DAVID LEMLEY DESIGN**
Designer: **DAVID LEMLEY DESIGN**
            SEATTLE, WASHINGTON

90   **DESIGNER'S COMMENTS:**
"Logo was created by painting in Photoshop and resampling image until semi-organic forms emerged. Final art was 300 dpi tiff."

Client: **DAVID LEMLEY DESIGN**
Designer: **DAVID LEMLEY DESIGN**
            SEATTLE, WASHINGTON

DESIGNER'S COMMENTS:
"Logo was created in FreeHand by autotracing typefaces repeatedly, then tweaking the results."

Client: **DAVID LEMLEY DESIGN**
Designer: DAVID LEMLEY DESIGN
SEATTLE, WASHINGTON

DESIGNER'S COMMENTS:
"Logo was created in FreeHand by rendering letterforms on top of each other until, out of the chaos, new letterforms emerged."

Client: **DAVID LEMLEY DESIGN**
Designer: DAVID LEMLEY DESIGN
SEATTLE, WASHINGTON

DESIGNER'S COMMENTS:
"Logo was created by scanning tissue of rough lettering into Photoshop and then applying ripple filter."

91

HEAVEN

Client: **DAVID LEMLEY DESIGN**
Designer: DAVID LEMLEY DESIGN
SEATTLE, WASHINGTON

Client: SEATTLE NEIGHBORHOOD GROUP
Designer: DAVID LEMLEY DESIGN
           SEATTLE, WASHINGTON

Client: DAVID LEMLEY DESIGN
Designer: DAVID LEMLEY DESIGN
           SEATTLE, WASHINGTON

DESIGNER'S COMMENTS:

92   *"Logo was created in FreeHand by rendering calligraphic letterforms with the pressure sensitive tool, controlling it with the arrows keys (as opposed to a wacom tablet) in order to achieve a deconstructionist feeling."*

Client: B-WILD
Designer: DAVID LEMLEY DESIGN
           SEATTLE, WASHINGTON

Client: DAVID LEMLEY DESIGN
Designer: DAVID LEMLEY DESIGN
SEATTLE, WASHINGTON

Client: CALLISON ARCHITECTURE
Designer: DAVID LEMLEY DESIGN
SEATTLE, WASHINGTON

Client: ALDUS
Designer: DAVID LEMLEY DESIGN
SEATTLE, WASHINGTON

Client: THE BON MARCHÉ
Designer: DAVID LEMLEY DESIGN
SEATTLE, WASHINGTON

Client: THE BON MARCHÉ
Designer: DAVID LEMLEY DESIGN
SEATTLE, WASHINGTON

94

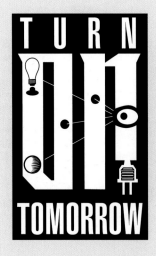

Client: THE BON MARCHÉ
Designer: DAVID LEMLEY DESIGN
SEATTLE, WASHINGTON

Client: **THE BON MARCHÉ**
Designer: **DAVID LEMLEY DESIGN**
(FOR LESLIE PHINNEY)
SEATTLE, WASHINGTON

PINE STREET
G O U R M E T

Client: **THE BON MARCHÉ**
Designer: **DAVID LEMLEY DESIGN**
SEATTLE, WASHINGTON

DESIGNER'S COMMENTS: 95
*"Logo was created in FreeHand using
vectors (points) and manipulating until
letterforms were perfect."*

Client: **THE BON MARCHÉ**
Designer: **DAVID LEMLEY DESIGN**
SEATTLE, WASHINGTON

Client: CATCH THE WAVE
Designer: TALBOT DESIGN GROUP
              WESTLAKE VILLAGE, CALIFORNIA

Client: WILMONT ASIA GROUP
Designer: DESIGN OBJECTIVES PTE LTD.
              SINGAPORE

96

Client: GREENSCREEN
Designer: CLIFFORD SELBERT DESIGN COLLABORATIVE
              CAMBRIDGE, MASSACHUSETTS

Client: GATEWAY SCHOOLS
Designer: KIKU OBATA & COMPANY
          ST. LOUIS, MISSOURI

Client: GREAT LAKES SCIENCE CENTER
Designer: KIKU OBATA & COMPANY
          ST. LOUIS, MISSOURI

97

Client: SEIKO INSTRUMENTS
Designer: 3 MARKETEERS ADVERTISING
          SAN JOSE, CALIFORNIA

XCENTURY

Client: **X-Century Studios**
Designer: SHIMOKOCHI/REEVES
LOS ANGELES, CALIFORNIA

Client: **La Rotonda sul Mare**
Designer: BRUCE YELASKA DESIGN
SAN FRANCISCO, CALIFORNIA

ROTONDA
SUL MARE

Autodesk Engineering

Client: **Autodesk**
Designer: BRUCE YELASKA DESIGN
SAN FRANCISCO, CALIFORNIA

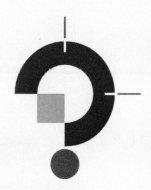

PIXEL INK
    DESKTOP PREPRESS
SOURCE

Client: PIXEL INK
Designer: BRUCE YELASKA DESIGN
        SAN FRANCISCO, CALIFORNIA

THE NATIONAL CONSUMER GUIDE

Client: CATALYST
Designer: BRUCE YELASKA DESIGN
        SAN FRANCISCO, CALIFORNIA

99

Client: UNIVERSITY OF CALIFORNIA
Designer: BRUCE YELASKA DESIGN
        SAN FRANCISCO, CALIFORNIA

STUDY CALIFORNIA

Client: ROCKINGHAM COUNCIL OF THE ARTS, INC.
Designer: SERAN DESIGN
            HARRISONBURG, VIRGINIA

DESIGNER'S COMMENTS:
"Fanfare was for a crafts, music, and foods festival. It portrays the fun and energetic festive scene by incorporating ribbons and confetti in the solid type. The logo was created using Adobe Illustrator 5.5 on Macintosh Quadra 700 computer.

"1. Fanfare was typed in Franklin Gothic Bold and sheared 20°. Then I used create outlines from the type menu to modify the letter forms.
2. The ribbons were created separately. The thicker one was created using the pen tool, then stylized with the calligraphy setting—pen width, 0.5 inch; pen angle, -120°—from the filter menu. The thinner one was created with the same process except for the calligraphy settings—pen width, 0.125 inch; pen angle, -120°.
3. The confetti was created using the rectangular tool, then rotated, and duplicated in places."

100

Client: BAYER CORPORATION
            AGFA DIVISION
Designer: THE HUGHES COMMUNICATIONS GROUP, INC.
            BOSTON, MASSACHUSETTS

Client: RICO PTE LTD.
Designer: DESIGN OBJECTIVES PTE LTD.
          SINGAPORE

SPECTRANET
INTERNATIONAL

Client: SPECTRANET INTERNATIONAL
Designer: LORENZ ADVERTISING & DESIGN, INC.
          SAN DIEGO, CALIFORNIA

Client: THE 1994 WORLD CUP SOCCER ASSOCIATION
Designer: EVENSON DESIGN GROUP
          CULVER CITY, CALIFORNIA

Client: **PRIVATE EXERCISE**
Designer: EVENSON DESIGN GROUP
              CULVER CITY, OHIO

Client: **STREAMLINE GRAPHICS**
Designer: EVENSON DESIGN GROUP
              CULVER CITY, CALIFORNIA

Client: **COLLEGE OF EDUCATION & PSYCHOLOGY**
JAMES MADISON UNIVERSITY
Designer: SERAN DESIGN
HARRISONBURG, VIRGINIA

DESIGNER'S COMMENTS:
*"'The two faces represent the focus of the College of Education and Psychology on
interaction between faculty and student, faculty and faculty, students and students,
and our graduates and the children and adults that they will eventually serve.'*

*"This logo was created using the pen tool in Adobe Illustrator 5.5 on Macintosh
Quadra 700 computer."*

103

Client: **DIGEX, INCORPORATED**
Designer: THE INVISIONS GROUP, LTD.
BETHESDA, MARYLAND

Client: **DEEP DESIGN**
Designer: STUDIO A
           ATLANTA, GEORGIA

Client: **DEEP DESIGN**
Designer: STUDIO A
           ATLANTA, GEORGIA

Client: **DEEP DESIGN**
Designer: STUDIO A
           ATLANTA, GEORGIA

Client: **DEEP DESIGN**
Designer: STUDIO A
           ATLANTA, GEORGIA

Client: JACON
           FASTENERS & ELECTRONICS
Designer: GRAFICA
           CANOGA PARK, CALIFORNIA

DESIGNER'S COMMENTS:
"Example of logo circa 1955 prior to update and redesign by Grafica"

Client: JACON
           FASTENERS & ELECTRONICS
Designer: GRAFICA
           CANOGA PARK, CALIFORNIA

Client: SurfPuppy Multimedia Group
Designer: SurfPuppy Multimedia Group
            Tulsa, Oklahaoma

Client: BB-Interactive
            John Beebe
Designer: Cawrse & Effect
            San Francisco, California

107

Client: Wisconisn Academy for Sciences, Arts and Letters
Designer: The Design Foundry
            Madison, Wisconsin

Client: **THE DESIGN FOUNDRY**
Designer: **THE DESIGN FOUNDRY**
MADISON, WISCONSIN

Client: **FUCH'S**
Designer: **MULLER + COMPANY**
KANSAS CITY, MISSOURI

Client: CONTINUUM COMPUTER CORPORATION
Designer: GRAFICA
          CANOGA PARK, CALIFORNIA

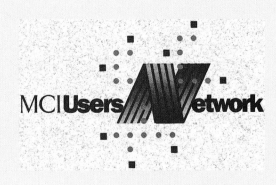

Client: MCI TELECOMMUNICATIONS CORPORATION
Designer: DEVER DESIGNS, INC.
          LAUREL, MARYLAND

109

Client: BLYTH SOFTWARE
Designer: GRAFICA
          CANOGA PARK, CALIFORNIA

Client: **DR. IRA WALLACE**
          LASER COSMETIC SURGERY
Designer: RANDI MARGRABIA DESIGN
          GLASSBORO, NEW JERSEY

Client: **NORTHWARD CONSTRUCTION**
Designer: GREG WELSH DESIGN
          SEATTLE, WASHINGTON

DESIGNER'S COMMENTS:
110 *"This was an attempt to evoke the feel of a California fruit crate label. Actual fruit crate labels were researched and some letterforms scanned, then redrawn in the computer. The wood grain was scanned from actual wood. While this would not have been impossible to create conventionally, it would have been much more difficult and time consuming."*

Client: THE GEORGE WASHINGTON UNIVERSITY
Designer: THE INVISIONS GROUP LTD.
          BETHESDA, MARYLAND

Client: SCORE AMERICA
Designer: LAURA COE DESIGN ASSOCIATES
          SAN DIEGO, CALIFORNIA

Client: GRAMERCY PICTURES
Designer: MIKE SALISBURY COMMUNICATIONS
          TORRANCE, CALIFORNIA

Client: **AMERICAN HOSPITAL ASSOCIATION**
SOCIETY FOR HEALTHCARE MANAGMENT
AND MARKET DEVELOPMENT
Designer: **COMCORP, INC.**
CHICAGO, ILLINOIS

Client: **ASIAN STUDIES CONFERENCE**
Designer: **SERAN DESIGN**
HARRISONBURG, VIRGINIA

DESIGNER'S COMMENTS:
"The Yin-Yang represents the Asian way of thinking. The logo tried to suggest the new active role of Asian-American scholars by adding dynamic motion to the Yin-Yang. The information surrounded by two vertical boxes and placed asymmetrically, resembling the bars of Iching, relates to Yin-Yang and makes the logo a piece of Asian art.

"This logo was created using Adobe Illustrator 5.5 on Macintosh Quadra 700 computer.

"1. The left side of the Yin-Yang was created using the pen tool, then flipped and duplicated horizontally.
2. The Yin-Yang was rotated -15°.
3. The information was typed in Stone Informal Semibold then centered.
4. The surrounded two vertical boxes
were created using the rectangular tool."

112

ASSOCIATION FOR ASIAN STUDIES

SOUTHEAST REGIONAL CONFERENCE

Designer: JAFAR NABKEL
BOULDER, COLORADO

IGNITION

Air Philippines

Client: AIR PHILIPPINES
Designer: DESIGN SYSTEMAT, INC.
          MAKATI CITY, PHILIPPINES

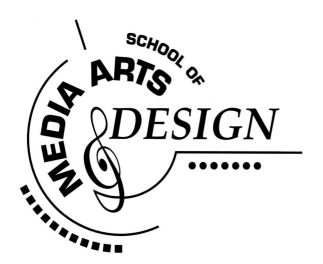

Client: JAMES MADISON UNIVERSITY
Designer: TRUDY COLE-ZIELANSKI DESIGN
            CHURCHVILLE, VIRGINIA

Client: J2 COLLECTION
Designer: THE DESIGN FOUNDRY
            MADISON, WISCONSIN

114

Client: INTERNET SERVICES INCORPORATED
Designer: MIND'S EYE DESIGN
            NEW ALBANY, INDIANA

Client: FEDERAL DATA CORPORATION
Designer: MACVICAR DESIGN AND COMMUNICATIONS
           ARLINGTON, VIRGINIA

Client: TALBOT EVENTS
Designer: TALBOT DESIGN GROUP
           WESTLAKE VILLAGE, CALIFORNIA

115

Client: JAMES MADISON UNIVERSITY
Designer: TRUDY COLE-ZIELANSKI DESIGN
           CHURCHVILLE, VIRGINIA

PAST DUE

Client: DOGSTAR "PAST DUE NOTICES"
Designer: DOGSTAR
           BIRMINGHAM, ALABAMA

116

PAST DUE

PAST DUE

Client: CLARK PRODUCTION SERVICES
Designer: PINPOINT COMMUNICATIONS
               DEERFIELD BEACH, FLORIDA

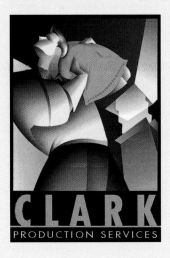

Client: GES EXPOSITION SERVICES
Designer: TIEKEN DESIGN & CREATIVE SERVICES
               PHOENIX, ARIZONA

Client: TALBOT DESIGN GROUP
               10TH ANNIVERSARY logo change
Designer: TALBOT DESIGN GROUP
               WESTLAKE VILLAGE, CALIFORNIA

Recreating the Revolution

NECC '94
Boston

Client: LESLEY COLLEGE
Designer: BARRETT COMMUNICATIONS
             CAMBRIDGE, MASSACHUSETTS

Client: ART CLASSICS LTD.
Designer: PHOENIX CREATIVE
             ST. LOUIS, MISSOURI

Client: AMARA HOTEL
Designer: DESIGN OBJECTIVES PTE LTD.
            SINGAPORE

Client: HEART OF AMERICA COUNCIL
            BOY SCOUTS OF AMERICA
Designer: MULLER + COMPANY   119
            KANSAS CITY, MISSOURI

Client: PHYSISPHERE
Designer: DEVER DESIGNS, INC.
            LAUREL, MARYLAND

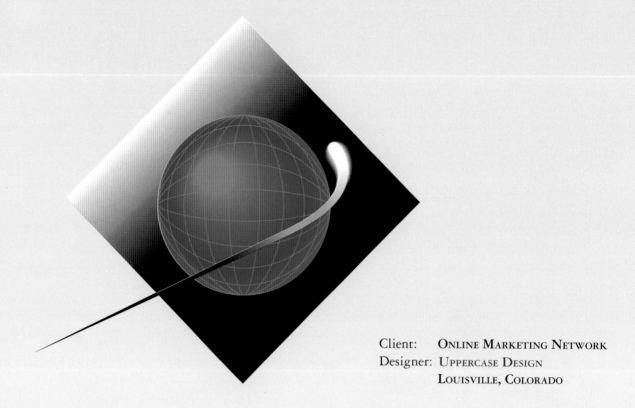

Client: ONLINE MARKETING NETWORK
Designer: UPPERCASE DESIGN
            LOUISVILLE, COLORADO

Client: TOKYO BROADCASTING SYSTEM—TBS
Designer: SHIMOKOCHI/REEVES
            LOS ANGELES, CALIFORNIA

Tokyo Broadcasting System

Client: NEON EDDY GLASSWORKS
Designer: GRAFICA
            CANOGA PARK, CALIFORNIA

Client: TRANS WORLD AIRLINES
            CAFE TWA
Designer: PHOENIX CREATIVE   121
            ST. LOUIS, MISSOURI

Client: VOYAGER FACTORY STORES
Designer: GRAFICA
            CANOGA PARK, CALIFORNIA

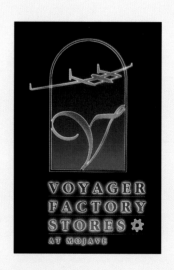

MUSIC/VIDEO

Client: **WHEREHOUSE ENTERTAINMENT**
Designer: **RETAIL PLANNING ASSOCIATES**
COLUMBUS, OHIO

Client: **CAMPBELL'S ENGINEERING**
Designer: **UPPERCASE DESIGN**
LOUISVILLE, COLORADO

DESIGNER'S COMMENTS:

122

"Campbell's is a precision custom machining, tool and die, welding and fabrication shop. The logo presents an image of precise and complex machining capability in the form of a constructed 'C'."

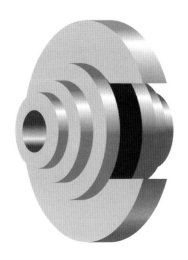

Client: **WHEREHOUSE ENTERTAINMENT**
Designer: **RETAIL PLANNING ASSOCIATES**
COLUMBUS, OHIO

Client: THE COCA-COLA COMPANY
Designer: DESGRIPPES GOBÉ & ASSOCIATES
               NEW YORK, NEW YORK

123

Client: WHEREHOUSE ENTERTAINMENT
Designer: RETAIL PLANNING ASSOCIATES
               COLUMBUS, OHIO

Client: **OUT SIDE IN**
Designer: **DF**ACTO
              BALBOA, CALIFORNIA

DESIGNER'S COMMENTS:
"A company that documents outdoor adventure experience in writing, photography, design, and multimedia publication."

Client: **HMC GRAPHIC DESIGN**
Designer: **HMC GRAPHIC DESIGN**
              NEW YORK, NEW YORK

DESIGNER'S COMMENTS:
"The HMC Graphic Design logo was created in Photoshop, Illustrator, and Quark XPress—printed as a 2-color logo.

"The main image (computer chip) was feathered several times to get the right fading effect. Then the defringe filter was used to create a more dispersing edge to the letters.

"The outline was created in Illustrator. The same letter characters were used as in the computer chip. Each letter was dissected enough to define the original face.

"The bar as well as the lettering beneath the logo was simply done in Quark XPress."

Client: MARRIOTT INTERNATIONAL, INC.
Designer: STEVE TRAPERO DESIGN
            SILVER SPRING, MARYLAND

DESIGNER'S COMMENTS:
"Giving the globe and computer mouse their 3-D appearance was achieved by adding radial gradients in Adobe Illustrator."

Client: 3DFX INTERACTIVE
Designer: SCOTT BROWN DESIGN
          REDWOOD CITY, CALIFORNIA

Client: ELECTRONIC BOOK TECHNOLOGIES
Designer: STEWART MONDERER DESIGN, INC.
BOSTON, MASSACHUSETTS

the GABRIEL *Consortium, inc.*

126

Client: THE GABRIEL CONSORTIUM, INC.
Designer: DEVER DESIGNS, INC.
LAUREL, MARYLAND

Client: BENCHMARK COMMUNICATIONS
Designer: MACVICAR DESIGN AND COMMUNICATIONS
ARLINGTON, VIRGINIA

Client: **MERISEL, INC.**
Designer: **MONNENS-ADDIS DESIGN**
BERKELEY, CALIFORNIA

Client: **COMFORT MOTORS PTE LTD.**
Designer: **DESIGN OBJECTIVES PTE LTD.**
SINGAPORE

127

Client: **MOTIVA SOFTWARE**
Designer: **LAURA COE DESIGN ASSOCIATES**
SAN DIEGO, CALIFORNIA

DESIGNER'S COMMENTS:
"Logo for a weight management software program for dieters. The mark conveys energy and health, which are the main-selling features of the product."

Client: **MAKE-A-WISH FOUNDATION OF AMERICA**
Designer: **TIEKEN DESIGN & CREATIVE SERVICES**
PHOENIX, ARIZONA

Client: **POTLATCH CORPORATION**
128 Designer: **PROFILE DESIGN**
SAN FRANCISCO, CALIFORNIA

Client: **CH2MHILL**
Designer: **YAMAMOTO MOSS**
MINNEAPOLIS, MINNESOTA

Client: BORDERS BOOKS AND MUSIC
Designer: FRCH DESIGN WORLDWIDE
          CINCINNATI, OHIO

Client: PRINTCOM PRINTING
Designer: UPPERCASE DESIGN
          LOUISVILLE, COLORADO

DESIGNER'S COMMENTS:
*"PrintCOM is a printing and communications firm
expanding to receive and distribute its printed matter
online. The logo combines a traditional offset press cylinder
with a sheet of paper coming off the press as well as
suggesting electronic input from the other direction."*

Client: **CHESEBROUGH-POND'S USA CO.**
Designer: HANS FLINK DESIGN INC.
NEW YORK, NEW YORK

Client: **HOFBAUER OF VIENNA LTD.**
Designer: HANS FLINK DESIGN INC.
NEW YORK, NEW YORK

130

Client: **CHESEBROUGH-POND'S USA CO.**
Designer: HANS FLINK DESIGN INC.
NEW YORK, NEW YORK

Client: **MOBERG EPSTEIN ARCHITECTS**
Designer: MICHAEL COURTNEY DESIGN
SEATTLE, WASHINGTON

Client: **DODSON GROUP**
Designer: MULLER + COMPANY
KANSAS CITY, MISSOURI

Client: **AMERICAN COLLEGE OF CARDIOLOGY**
Designer: STEVE TRAPERO DESIGN
BETHESDA, MARYLAND

DESIGNER'S COMMENTS:
"Radial and lineal gradients, and layering were used to give this logo depth and an upscale feel."

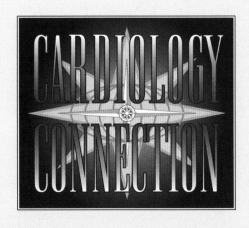

Client: **BARKLEY COMPANY OF ARIZONA**
Designer: **LORENZ ADVERTISING & DESIGN, INC.**
           SAN DIEGO, CALIFORNIA

Client: **GOWAN COMPANY**
Designer: **LORENZ ADVERTISING & DESIGN, INC.**
           SAN DIEGO, CALIFORNIA

Atlanta Botanical Garden

Plants do the Wildest THINGS

SELF-GUIDED TOUR

¹³³

Client: ATLANTA BOTANICAL GARDENS
Designer: CokerGolley Limited
          ATLANTA, GEORGIA

Client: WHITMYER BIOMECHANIX
Designer: SYNERGY DESIGN GROUP
          TALLAHASSEE, FLORIDA

POSSUM
P R O D U C T S

REEL CITY
PRODUCTIONS

Client: **REEL CITY PRODUCTIONS**
Designer: **MONNENS-ADDIS DESIGN**
BERKELEY, CALIFORNIA

Client: **THERMOSCAN**

Designer: **MIRES DESIGN**
SAN DIEGO, CALIFORNIA

Client: **CORPORATE COMMUNICTIONS, INC.**
Designer: **STEWART MONDERER DESIGN, INC.**
BOSTON, MASSACHUSETTS

Client: NuThena
Designer: MacVicar Design and Communications
             Arlington, Virginia

DESIGNER'S COMMENTS:
"NuThena is a company specializing in computer modeling and related software.

"The mark was created in Adobe Illustrator 5.0, using precise linework on a tight grid. The letterforms were created and minutely adjusted on the computer."

135

Client: IMAGE GATE
Designer: Z•D STUDIOS
             Madison, Wisconsin

DESIGNER'S COMMENTS:
"Image Gate is a 16mm film camera rental company.

"My vision was to marry the mediums and create a printed mark that echoed the film directors' higher visual standards of their media over that of the video directors' media. It needed to have the rich, raw visual quality of 16mm film.

"First the Image Gate text was created in Adobe Illustrator and imaged on a 300 dpi laserwriter. I took an X-acto blade and scraped the toner to create a distressed look to the letterforms. From there the black and white image was blown up on a Xerox and scanned into my system on an Agfa Arcus scanner, retouched in Photoshop and output to fill an 8.5 x 11 page. After that, I painted that exact printed text onto a piece of glass with India Ink, attached that to a stand, placed a canvas behind it and projected its shadow onto the canvas. We then shot 16mm film of the image while the canvas was being moved in a 'wave-like' motion. That film was developed and I selected a portion of the footage, scanned that into my Macintosh system, created a duotone of black and gold metallic, then designed the letterhead. The logo portion was cropped in Photoshop and the word 'FILM' was created and given a radius, lasso tool blur."

NEW YORK–SWITZERLAND ENTERPRISE

Client: New York-Switzerland Enterprise
Designer: Hans Flink Design Inc.
          New York, New York

Client: SPCI
Designer: MacVicar Design and Communications
          Arlington, Virginia

Client: Bayer Corporation
Designer: Hans Flink Design Inc.
          New York, New York

600 WATERGATE

Client: 600 WATERGATE
Designer: MACVICAR DESIGN AND COMMUNICATIONS
ARLINGTON, VIRGINIA

DESIGNER'S COMMENTS:
"The building has very distinctive architecture that is reflected in the symbol.

"The mark was created in Adobe Illustrator 5.0, using precise linework on a tight grid. One element was rendered, moved and repeated, and then scaled to create the feel of a three-dimensional building in perspective."

137

Client: UPS WORLDWIDE LOGISTICS
Designer: DEEP DESIGN
ATLANTA, GEORGIA

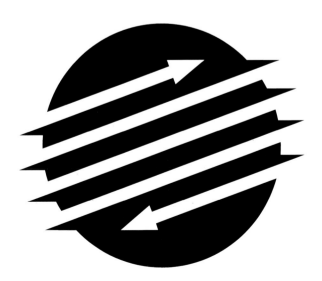

Client: JUICE WORKS JUICE BAR
Designer: TIEKEN DESIGN & CREATIVE SERVICES
              PHOENIX, ARIZONA

Client: THE FISHIN' PLACE
138 Designer: TEAMDESIGN, INC.
              SEATTLE, WASHINGTON

Client: ST. LOUIS SPORTS COMMISSION
Designer: PHOENIX CREATIVE
              ST. LOUIS, MISSOURI

Client: LITTLE CITY
           CARRY OUT SECTION
Designer: BRUCE YELASKA DESIGN
           SAN FRANCISCO, CALIFORNIA

Client: NFL PROPERTIES
           NEW ENGLAND PATRIOTS
Designer: EVENSON DESIGN GROUP   139
           CULVER CITY, CALIFORNIA

Client: LE CAR PTE LTD.
Designer: DESIGN OBJECTIVES PTE LTD.
           SINGAPORE

Client: INDUSTRY PICTURES
Designer: MIRES DESIGN
　　　　　SAN DIEGO, CALIFORNIA

Client: McGRAW HILL
Designer: MIRES DESIGN
　　　　　SAN DIEGO, CALIFORNIA

Client: FUSION MEDIA
Designer: MIRES DESIGN
　　　　　SAN DIEGO, CALIFORNIA

Client: BAY•T GRAPHIC DESIGN
Designer: BAY•T GRAPHIC DESIGN
               CORONA, CALIFORNIA

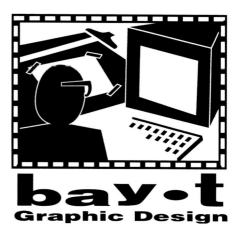

Client: ARONOFF CENTER
Designer: FRCH DESIGN WORLDWIDE
               (FORMERLY SDI/HTI)   141
               NEW YORK, NEW YORK

Client: PADI
Designer: BAY•T GRAPHIC DESIGN
               CORONA, CALIFORNIA

PHAMIS
INCORPORATED

Client: PHAMIS, INCORPORATED
Designer: PHINNEY/BISCHOFF DESIGN HOUSE
             SEATTLE, WASHINGTON

Client: PARAMOUNT PICTURES THEME PARKS
Designer: VISUAL MARKETING ASSOCIATES, INC.
             DAYTON, OHIO

142   **DESIGNER'S COMMENTS:**

"We began with a 'special/plasma' image and gave it some hurricane-like motion, to suck you into the visual experience. And, since development for the mark was well in advance of the construction, we illustrated the tracks from blueprints and Polaroid pictures of similar rubular coasters, first in Macromedia FreeHand, then rendered in Aldus Photoshop. The 'Flight of Fear' typography was also initialized in FreeHand, then taken into Photoshop and given a motion blur as well (as an 'alienish' glow) to convey the element of being pulled rapidly into the unknown.

"The most challenging part of this project was translating a four-color process logo into one-, two-, and three-color versions for various production needs, such as embroidery or screenprinting."

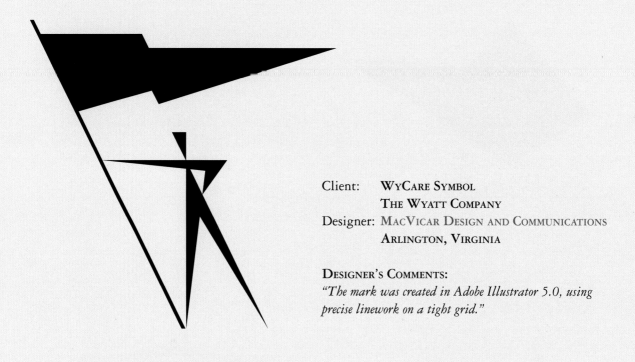

Client: **WyCare Symbol**
The Wyatt Company
Designer: **MacVicar Design and Communications**
Arlington, Virginia

Designer's Comments:
*"The mark was created in Adobe Illustrator 5.0, using
precise linework on a tight grid."*

Client: **Newsletter Services**
Designer: **MacVicar Design and Communications**
Arlington, Virginia

Designer's Comments:
*"The mark was created in Adobe Illustrator 5.0, using
precise linework on a tight grid."*

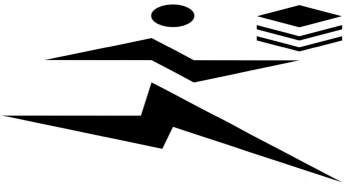

CAPSTONE™
INDUSTRIES

Client: **CAPSTONE INDUSTRIES**
Designer: **PINPOINT COMMUNICATIONS**
DEERFIELD BEACH, FLORIDA

Client: **LOTUS LANE RACING TEAM**
144 Designer: **MULLER + COMPANY**
KANSAS CITY, MISSOURI

Client: **BUCKHEAD LIFE RESTAURANT GROUP**
Designer: **ANTISTA FAIRCLOUGH DESIGN**
ATLANTA, GEORGIA

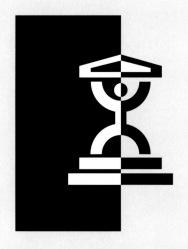 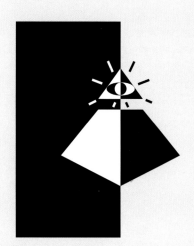 

Client: CONNIE LEE
            (CONSTRUCTION FINANCE SYMBOLS)
Designer: MACVICAR DESIGN AND COMMUNICATIONS
            ARLINGTON, VIRGINIA

DESIGNER'S COMMENTS:
"The mark was created in Adobe Illustrator 5.0, using precise linework on a tight grid. The symbols were rendered and then a filter was used to create the positive/negative effect."

Client: LittleTreasures Child Care Center
Designer: Trudy Cole-Zielanski Design
Churchville, Virginia

Client: Citizens Against Sexual Assault
Designer: Trudy Cole-Zielanski Design
Churchville, Virginia

146

Building Community
one person
at a Time

Client: Dayton Nursery School
Designer: Trudy Cole-Zielanski Design
Churchville, Virginia

Client: THE SEMINOLE TRIBE OF FLORIDA PUBLICATIONS
Designer: SYNERGY DESIGN GROUP
TALLAHASSEE, FLORIDA

Client: THE UNIVERSITY CLUB
Designer: CATHEY ASSOCIATES, INC.
DALLAS, TEXAS

DESIGNER'S COMMENTS:
"This logo was designed in Adobe Illustrator and executed in both Illustrator and Adobe Photoshop. When lithographed on paper, the logo is normally printed in two spot colors, and the background of the central illustration, executed as a duotone in Photoshop, is 'placed' within the Illustrator document as an EPS image. Illustrator's masking function is used to control the exact shape and placement of the sun-ray halo."

147

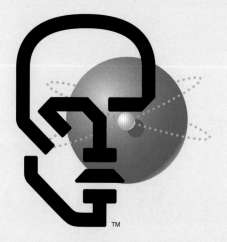

Client: **CST IMAGES**
Designer: LORENZ ADVERTISING & DESIGN, INC.
SAN DIEGO, CALIFORNIA

CST Images

Client: BIRMINGHAM JUNIOR LEAGUE
CHARGE INTO READING
Designer: DOGSTAR
BIRMINGHAM, ALABAMA

Client: UNITED STATES INSTITUTE OF PEACE
             VIRTUAL DIPLOMACY SYMBOL
Designer: MACVICAR DESIGN AND COMMUNICATIONS
             ARLINGTON, VIRGINIA

DESIGNER'S COMMENTS:
"The mark was created in Adobe Illustrator 5.0, using precise linework on a tight grid. The symmetrical elements were copied and flipped. The artwork was duplicated on top of itself and different strokes and fills were used to create the separate outlines."

149

Client: NEWELL OFFICE PRODUCTS
Designer: THE DESIGN FOUNDRY
             MADISON, WISCONSIN

Client: **H.O.L.A.** Recodings L.L.C.
Designer: Ron Kellum
New York, New York

150 Client: **Interex**
Designer: Insight Design Communications
Wichita, Kansas

Designer's comments:
"Interex manufactures innovative computer equipment.

"The X with the arrows pointing in and out simultaneously and the type were created in Freehand 5.5, exported into Illustrator and opened in Photoshop 3.0.5.

"In Photoshop, multiple filters were applied on multiple layers. Layer 1 was a solid blue rectangle with reversed out X. Layer 2 was a grayscale of layer 1 with GE chrome filter applied, opacity at 35% and layer mode on multiply. Layer 3 was a duplicate of layer 1 with Paint Alchemy filter applied and opacity at 60%. Layer 4 was a shadow of the Interex type while layer 5 was the Interex type itself."

Custom Rug Design

Client: UNIFICATIONS
Designer: CATHEY ASSOCIATES, INC.
               DALLAS, TEXAS

DESIGNER'S COMMENTS:

"This logo was designed and executed in Adobe Illustrator. The bold type characters began as a type font with the word, 'Unifications' typed on the computer's keyboard. The characters were first converted to outlines, making each a separate 'drawn' object. Then they were repositioned into their overlapping relationships. They were cut into the various 'jigsaw' shapes for the visual colors by Illustrator's divide plug-in filter. The logo is normally printed in only two spot colors with the lightest overlap areas being light halftone screens of both the printing colors. This screening of the two colors negates any need for trapping either color. For sample books and signage, the logo is screen-printed in three colors."

Client: EGAD!
               ELECTRONIC GRAPHIC ARTISTS OF DALLAS
Designer: CATHEY ASSOCIATES, INC.
               DALLAS, TEXAS

DESIGNER'S COMMENTS:

"EGAD! is a Macintosh user group for professional graphic artists and designers. This logo began as an effort to produce something simple and elegant that implied the need for a computer in the execution. It was executed in Adobe Illustrator with two gradient fills which establish the 'computerized' nature of the logo and the user group. The large letters and the dots reversing out of them are actually one single drawn object filled with a gradient and placed in front of a simple rectangle filled with another gradient."

ELECTRONIC GRAPHIC ARTISTS OF DALLAS

Client: TEXAS TIMING SYSTEMS
Designer: CATHEY ASSOCIATES, INC.
                 DALLAS, TEXAS

DESIGNER'S COMMENTS:
"This logo for a cross country race timing firm was designed and executed in Adobe Illustrator. Aside from controlling the symmetrical geometry of the 'star man', Illustrator provided control of the type around the circle with the application's text on path function."

Client: TELECELLULAR, INC.
Designer: CATHEY ASSOCIATES, INC.
                 DALLAS, TEXAS

DESIGNER'S COMMENTS:
"This logo was designed and executed in Adobe Illustrator. During the rough design process, the application made simple work of bending the geometry of the shapes to match each other in a variety of configurations."

Advanced Network Technologies, Inc.

Advanced Network Technologies, Inc.

Client: ADVANCED NETWORK TECHNOLOGIES, INC.
Designer: CATHEY ASSOCIATES, INC.
          DALLAS, TEXAS

DESIGNER'S COMMENTS:
"This logo was designed and executed in Adobe Illustrator. The thin lines are simple stroked paths which cause a slight complication in placing the logo over colored backgrounds. The stroke color must be altered to match each background. Experiments with cutting the lines out of the four colored areas proved to be less successful, due to the thin weight of the lines. The logo's complicated nature in its full-color form required the development of a second version for low resolution or small monochrome uses. The low res version has the tones of the logo's four divisions described with varying weights of reversed lines which in this case, are actually cut out of the logo."

PROTOCOL

Client: PROTOCOL
             INTERNATIONAL BUSINESS COMMUNICATIONS
Designer: KIMURA DESIGN
             ANCHORAGE, ALASKA

Client: UNIFICATIONS
Designer: CATHEY ASSOCIATES, INC.
             DALLAS, TEXAS

154   **DESIGNER'S COMMENTS:**
"This logo for a data processing service bureau was designed and executed in Adobe Illustrator. The 'data cluster' of small squares blending into the 'TAB' were refined from a full grid of complete squares. The squares were selectively hidden and shown until the most pleasing grouping was selected. The unused squares were simply deleted."

Client: **RADCOM**
Designer: CATHEY ASSOCIATES, INC.
           DALLAS, TEXAS

DESIGNER'S COMMENTS:
"This logo was designed and executed in Adobe Illustrator. The shading of the globe in the center was done with an object blend which provided more control of the shape and tones of the shading than would have been easily accomplished with a gradient fill."

Client: **SECOND OPINION INTERIORS**
Designer: CATHEY ASSOCIATES, INC.
           DALLAS, TEXAS

DESIGNER'S COMMENTS:
"This logo was designed and executed in Adobe Illustrator. The design started as two tones of gray with a very flat look. The decision to go for three-dimensional shading actually came late in the design process. Since the stationery was to be printed in only two colors, the design offered a challenge in getting two spot colors to balance with each other in one 'ball'. Two individual balls were developed with gradient fills to show the third dimension. After the logo shapes were excised from each ball, the intensities of the two spot colors were established to achieve a unified look. For color traps, the lighter color must be spread across the 'S' line where the colors meet. This is accomplished by offsetting the path of the lighter color's area and assigning overprint to its fill.

The logo works well in gray tones, but for low-res monochromatic uses, such as foil stamping on small ad specialities, a flat version with no gradation and with a thin outline around the upper right section had to be developed. For a full process color version, The Illustrator file is opened in Adobe Photoshop and saved in CMYK mode."

The Joiner-Rose Group, Inc.

Acoustical Engineers & Architects

Client: THE JOINER-ROSE GROUP, INC.
Designer: CATHEY ASSOCIATES, INC.
             DALLAS, TEXAS

DESIGNER'S COMMENTS:
"This logo was designed and executed in Adobe Illustrator. Following the establishments of the best relationships between the various line weights and line spacings, achieving the geometric symmetry was as simple as duplicating and rotating a completed half of the design."

Client: INTEGRATED CONCEPTS
Designer: CATHEY ASSOCIATES, INC.
             DALLAS, TEXAS

DESIGNER'S COMMENTS:
"This logo was designed and executed in Adobe Illustrator employing the application's great mathematical control of geometric designs."

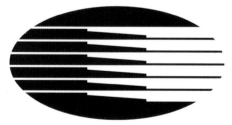

Integrated Concepts
INCORPORATED

Client: STARCK 2000 S.A.
Designer: KATUN CORPORATION
            MINNEAPOLIS, MINNESOTA

Client: VIRTUAL LINE
Designer: CATHEY ASSOCIATES, INC.
            DALLAS, TEXAS

157

DESIGNER'S COMMENTS:
*"This logo was designed in Adobe Illustrator and executed
in both Illustrator and Adobe Photoshop. The globe, the
line, and the type reading 'Virtual Line' were first drawn
in Illustrator for tight control of the shapes of the areas.
Each of the three major parts was saved as a separate
black and white illustration from Illustrator and reopened
by Photoshop. In Photoshop the parts were reassembled as
individual channels in a new file. Each channel was then
used to apply the visual treatments, and all three were
combined to establish the drop shadow which was shifted
and softened with a blur. The smaller type, 'Corporate
Internet Services', was executed in Illustrator for crispness,
and the main logo illustration from Photoshop was placed
within that same Illustrator file as an EPS image to
complete the logo."*

RESONATE

Client: RESONATE
Designer: SCOTT BROWN DESIGN
REDWOOD CITY, CALIFORNIA

Client: AXXYS TECHNOLOGIES
Designer: CATHEY ASSOCIATES, INC.
DALLAS, TEXAS

DESIGNER'S COMMENTS:
"This logo was designed and executed in Adobe Illustrator. Each one of the red swirls was individually drawn with the pen tool. They began as slightly larger objects with white outlines to help establish good spacing between them. The outlines were converted to drawn objects with the outline stroked path filter and cut out from the red swirls with the minus front filter. For symmetry, the red swirls were then duplicated and rotated to form the black swirls."

CatheyAssociates,Inc.
Graphic Design & Identity Development

Client: CATHEY ASSOCIATES, INC.
Designer: CATHEY ASSOCIATES, INC.
           DALLAS, TEXAS

DESIGNER'S COMMENTS:
"This logo was designed and executed in Adobe Illustrator. All the dots were originally the same size and arranged on an equally spaced grid which was rotated 45°. They were then individually resized, anchoring on the center of each, in incremental steps to achieve the optical illusion of a stylized 'C' emerging from a coarse halftone screen. For a bolder look, the type characters of the company name were 'fattened' by Illustrator's offset path filter after they were converted from font characters to outlines."

Client: ONE SOURCE COMMUNICATIONS, INC.
Designer: CATHEY ASSOCIATES, INC.
           DALLAS, TEXAS

DESIGNER'S COMMENTS:
"This logo was designed and executed in Adobe Illustrator. The large red 'O' actually started as a solid area with no 'doughnut hole'. The star burst was then cut out of the three red characters. This successful design results from one of the best attributes of electronic drawing programs— many logo variations can be developed in a very short time, allowing the designer to reduce his experimentation time and to show as many options to the client as desired."

Finished Art inc.

Client: FINISHED ART INC.
Designer: FINISHED ART INC.
            ATLANTA, GEORGIA

DESIGNER'S COMMENTS:
*"A new corporate image began with a symbolic graphic
derived from the studio initials. That basic format,
presented as a blank canvas to all 16 staff artists,
exploded into 48 full-color illustrated interpretations.
Illustrators and designers used traditional media such as
watercolors, pastels, and airbrush, as well as computer-
created art in several software programs to express
individual visions of the graphic shape. The results are a
mini-portfolio showing cartoons, realistic illustrations,
photomontages, abstract patterns, and symbolic graphics.
These images are printed as self-adhesive stickers (pp. 162
&163) that are used to personalize individual business
cards and are also used as studio identity stickers on work
delivered to clients. This creative process continues with
new applications developing such as holiday greetings
(right), an anniversary sticker (p. 161), lobby exhibit (p.
161), and more to come."*

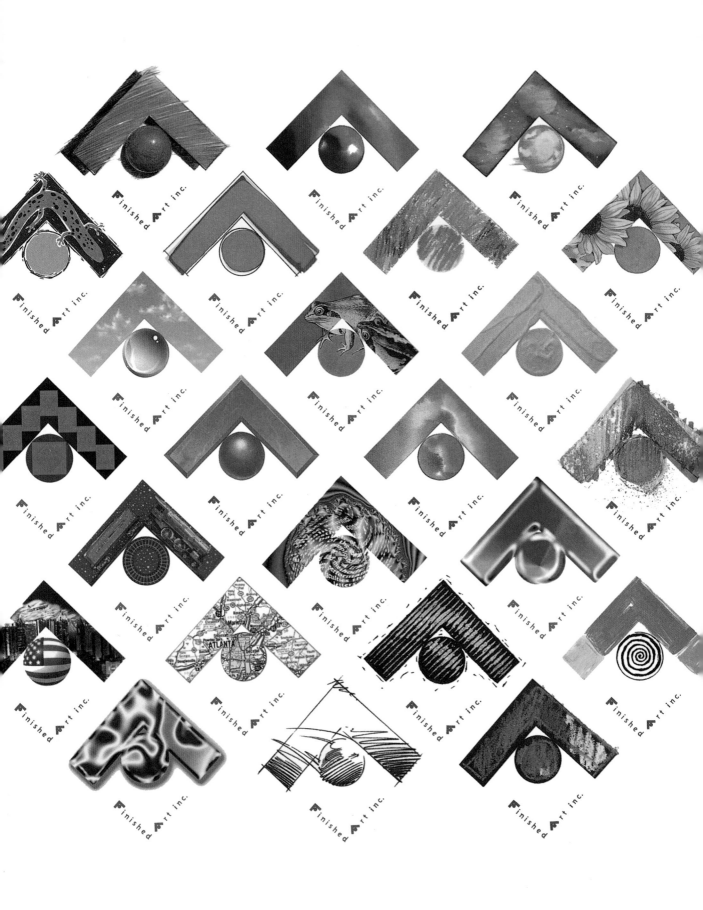

Pyramid Health

Client: PYRAMID HEALTH
Designer: ADAM, FILIPPO & ASSOCIATES, INC.
           PITTSBURGH, PENNSYLVANIA

Client: VERUS
Designer: FUNK & ASSOCIATES
           EUGENE, OREGON

164

Client: TRUST BANK
Designer: RASSMAN DESIGN
           DENVER, COLORADO

TRUST BANK OF COLORADO

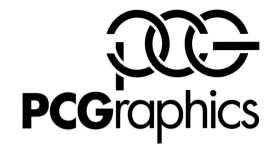

Client: **PCGraphics**
Designer: Randi Margrabia Design
          Glassboro, New Jersey

Client: Germersheim Central
Designer: Finished Art Inc.
          Atlanta, Georgia

Client: **BANANAPPEAL**
Designer: **FINISHED ART INC.**
          ATLANTA, GEORGIA

Client: **ORION**
Designer: **FINISHED ART INC.**
          ATLANTA, GEORGIA

Client: COCA-COLA
Designer: FINISHED ART INC.
            ATLANTA, GEORGIA

167

Client: COCA-COLA
Designer: FINISHED ART INC.
            ATLANTA, GEORGIA

Client: **GRANT BROTHERS**
Designer: **COMMUNICATION ARTS, INC.**
BOULDER, COLORADO

Client: **CLUB CAR CAFE**
Designer: **KIKU OBATA & COMPANY**
ST. LOUIS, MISSOURI

FannieMae

Client: FANNIE MAE
Designer: THE INVISIONS GROUP LTD.
          AUSTIN, TEXAS

Client: BROKERS NATIONAL LIFE ASSURANCE COMPANY
Designer: GRAPHIC EDGE, INC.
          AUSTIN, TEXAS

169

Client: THE NORTHWEST MOUNTAIN SCHOOL
Designer: THE INVISIONS GROUP LTD.
            BETHESDA, MARYLAND

170

Client: OTTO (RESTAURANT)
Designer: FYFE DESIGN
            CAMBRIDGE, MASSACHUSETTS

otto

AUSTIN AQUA FESTIVAL

35TH ANNIVERSARY

Client:　　AUSTIN AQUA FESTIVAL
Designer: GRAPHIC EDGE, INC.
　　　　　AUSTIN, TEXAS

Client:　　FURMAN & FURMAN ARCHITECTS
Designer: EPIGRAPH STUDIOS INC.
　　　　　NEW YORK, NEW YORK

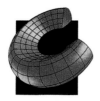

CAD/CAM CONSULTING SERVICES INC.
SALES · SERVICE · SUPPORT

Client: CAD CAM CONSULTING SERVICES, INC.
Designer: TALBOT DESIGN GROUP
              WESTLAKE VILLAGE, CALIFORNIA

172

Client: RUBIN MARKETING COMMUNICATIONS
Designer: DEEP DESIGN
            ATLANTA, GEORGIA

Client: NATIONAL ASSOCIATION OF STATE DEPARTMENTS OF AGRICULTURE
            INTERNATIONAL FOOD EXPORT SHOW
Designer: MACVICAR AND COMMUNICATIONS
            ARLINGTON, VIRGINIA

DESIGNER'S COMMENTS:
"The mark was created in Adobe Illustrator 5.0, using precise linework on a tight grid. The central artwork was duplicated on top of itself and moved. White fills on top of black fills created the unique shadow effect against the striped background."

Client: LASALLE PARTNERS
            633 ST. CLAIR
Designer: COMCORP, INC.
            CHICAGO, ILLINOIS

633 St. Clair

Client: THE PHOENIX ZOO
Designer: PAPAGALOS AND ASSOCIATES
           PHOENIX, ARIZONA

174

Client: FRASER PAPER
Designer: MCKNIGHT KURLAND
           CHICAGO, ILLINOIS

Client: CITY BREWERY INVESTMENTS CORPORATION
Designer: DESIGN SERVICES, INC.
           BATON ROUGE, LOUISIANA

175

Client: PELE'S CATERING COMPANY
Designer: GOSS KELLER MARTINEZ, INC.
DEL MAR, CALIFORNIA

Client: LIVEWORKS, INC.
176 Designer: THE STEPHENZ GROUP
SAN JOSE, CALIFORNIA

Client: SCOTT FORESMAN-ADDISON WESLEY
Designer: GOSS KELLER MARTINEZ, INC.
DEL MAR, CALIFORNIA

electronic education

(...no, they don't make logos like they used to!)